Stained Glass

A Beginners Guide To Stunning Stained Glass Methods, Techniques & Projects

1st Edition

By Olive Montgums

© **Copyright 2017 by Olive Montgums. All rights reserved.**

This document is geared towards providing exact and reliable information in regards to the topic and issue covered. The publication is sold with the idea that the publisher is not required to render accounting, officially permitted, or otherwise, qualified services. If advice is necessary, legal or professional, a practiced individual in the profession should be ordered.

- From a Declaration of Principles which was accepted and approved equally by a Committee of the American Bar Association and a Committee of Publishers and Associations.

In no way is it legal to reproduce, duplicate, or transmit any part of this document in either electronic means or in printed format. Recording of this publication is strictly prohibited and any storage of this document is not allowed unless with written permission from the publisher. All rights reserved.

The information provided herein is stated to be truthful and consistent, in that any liability, in terms of inattention or otherwise, by any usage or abuse of any policies, processes, or directions contained within is the solitary and utter responsibility of the recipient reader. Under no circumstances will any legal responsibility or blame be held against the publisher for any reparation, damages, or monetary loss due to the information herein, either directly or indirectly.

Respective authors own all copyrights not held by the publisher.

The information herein is offered for informational purposes solely, and is universal as so. The presentation of the information is without contract or any type of guarantee assurance.

Table of Contents

Introduction 1

Chapter 1 – Getting Started 4

   Stained Glass Crafting Tools 5

   Foil versus Lead 23

Chapter 2- The Process 25

   Step 1: Choosing the Pattern 27

   Step 2: Creating the Template 28

   Step 3: Scoring and Cutting the Glass 30

   Step 4: Grinding the Edges 35

   Step 5: Applying Copper Foil or Lead Came. 38

      Copper Foiling 39

      Lead Came 43

   Step 6: Soldering 51

      Soldering Foil 51

      Soldering Lead Came 56

   Step 7: Finishing 58

      Cleaning 58

      Applying Patina 61

Chapter 3 –Stained Glass – Painting 64

   Tools and Materials: 65

   Making Stained Glass – Painting 71

- Step 1- Cleaning the Glass 71
- Step 2: Creating the Outline 72
- Step 3A: Filling in with Color 77
- Step 3B: Matting 78

Chapter 4 – Beginner Projects 82

- Stained Glass Box 82
  - Materials and Tools: 82
  - What to do: 84
- Suncatcher 90
  - Materials and Tools: 90
  - What to Do 92
- Lampshade 95
  - Materials and Tools: 95
  - What to do: 96
- Conclusion 105

Introduction

First of all I'd like to thank you for purchasing the book *"Stained Glass: A Beginners Guide To Stunning Stained Glass Methods, Techniques & Projects"*.

For centuries, people have been awed by the almost magical effect of stained glass. Whether the panes are in a majestic medieval church or a comfortable home, there's no denying this work of art is a site to behold. How can one not be enthralled by these intricately designed patterns that seem to come to life as the lighting changes?

This book contains all the essential information beginners would need to create their own stained glass masterpiece. From tools and materials required to step by step instructions on basic projects to get you started, this book is the ultimate guide to stained glass making.

"Stained Glass: A Beginners Guide To Stunning Stained Glass Methods, Techniques & Projects " contains the following sections:

I. **Getting Started** – Detailed information on everything you need to work on projects.

II. **Techniques** – Provides information on all the method and techniques needed to make stained glass.

III. **Projects** – Step by step guides on projects that a beginner can use to create his or her own work of art.

Stained Glass making is a craft that requires a lot of patience. But the end result is certainly worth all the time and effort that you put in. So, remember to take note of the tips included in this book and give yourself time to get used to the techniques, and you'll be rewarded with the most enchanting stained glass projects.

Thank you for purchasing this book, I hope you enjoy it!

Chapter 1 – Getting Started

Over a thousand years ago, artists discovered a form of painting that was done on glass instead of regular canvas. At that time, silver stains were applied to the glass panels used for windows. Theses stains were put on the side of the glass that would be facing the outside. This technique softened the light that would come in through the windows. Artists took advantage of this method and added other colors to enhance the effect.

Stained glass windows were the craze for churches during the medieval period. It was when the gothic style was celebrated by most artists. The intricately designed windows depicted religious symbols such as the cross, the holy trinity and the saints.

When the Renaissance period came, stained glass did not go out the proverbial window as most gothic elements did. In the 1400's, glass panels became more affordable so this art form became available for other applications. Stained glass windows were added to private homes. These were used to show coat of arms and scenes related to the family's history.

In the centuries that followed, folks found various uses for stained glass. These creative panels were no longer limited to just windows. Lamps and fireplace screens are just some of the new uses for the colorful glass.

Stained Glass Crafting Tools

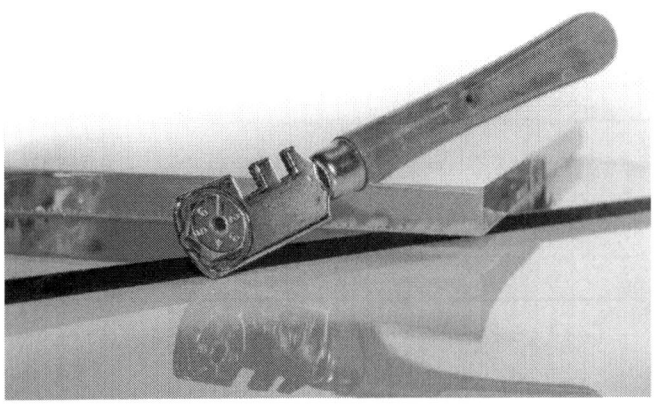

Before you can start working on stained glass projects, you need to make sure that you have the necessary tools. Some of these tools may be a little bit pricey but certainly are a worthy investment if you want to get started with stained glass.

1. **Glass** – Obviously, you will need glass for your projects. There are 2 basic types of glass that you can choose from to use in crafting stained glass. They are:

   - **Cathedral glass** also referrred to as Transparent glass is clear. It is highly translucent so you can see through it. This quality means that there's also a larger amount of light that can pass through the glass.

   - **Opalescent glass** has a milky appearance that's caused by the white opal that is incorporated into the pane. The opaque quality depends on the amount of opal in the mixture. The more opal the less translucent it is. This type of glass is great for keeping out harsh light.

   Both types come in a variety of colors and textures. However, as a beginner it is best to start off with clear glass that's used for windows. This is easy to find and available at your local hardware store.

   Clear window glass is less expensive so you don't have to worry about breaking the bank as you learn the different techniques needed. Once you are more familiar with the techniques used in crafting, you can start working with the more expensive glass.

Using the 2 basic types mentioned above, there are probably hundreds of glass sub types that you can choose from. Below are some of the most commonly used,

- **Full Antique** – This type of glass is handmade and gets its name from the method used to create it. A full antique glass is made using the historical mouth blowing technique that has been used since the old days.

  Full antiques are characterized by small round bubbles and beautiful linear striations. It is perfect for almost any type of project. You can use it as the background or the design detail. However, because of the intricate process used in making it, full antique glass is quite expensive.

- **Drawn Antique** (a.k.a semi-antique, new antique or machine antique)- This type of glass is less expensive than full antique as it is made using a machine. The quality though is almost as exquisite as its pricier counterpart. It features the same attractive linear striations but does not have the uniqe bubbles or seeds. It is ideal to use as background, border or as a full panel.

- **Scribed Antique** – This is a special texture designed in 1996 by Spectrum Glass. The design is trademarked under the name Artique and features the same elements as a full antique. The main difference is that it is machine made with the antique identifying features such as the striations deliberately scribed on the surface of the hot glass.

  It is best used as a border, background, and as full panels. It costs much less than full antique, which makes it a popular choice amongst stained glass craftsmen. The only drawback is that it is only available from the company it is trademarked under.

- **Bevels** – This type of glass produces a prism-like lighting effect. And this is because of the way it is shaped or formed. Bevels are thick glass plates with ground down edges so the center is embossed or raised at an angle other than 90 degrees. This unique physical characteristic allows light that passes through the glass to be refracted to create the almost magical lighting effect.

You can find this type of glass in different shapes and sizes to fit your design or project. These are best used as borders but can of course be incorporated into the pattern you are creating.

- **Baroque** – This is another type of glass that is trademarked by Specttrum Glass. It has a swirly 3D texture that gives the design some element of movement. So, if you're creating something that includes the sky, a body of water or even grass, this is the best type to use.

However, the swirly texture can be a bit challenging to work with especially for a beginner. You need to consider the direction of the swirls for each piece or panel that you use to ensure that your pattern is cohesive. Mismatched swirls may result in a chaotic appearance.

- **Catspaw** – If you have ever seen what a glass surface looks like when a cat decides to walk on it, then you know exactly what the texture on this type of glass looks like. The pattern on the texture is created by hot glass being chilled on a cool surface.

It is ideal for designs where you need to create a contrasting texture from the background. If your stained glass pattern includes flowers and trees, you can use catspaw to make the petals and trunks stand out.

- **Crackle glass** - This type of glass is one of the more expensive variety. It is made the same way full antique is created, through the mouth blowing method. The slight difference is that the hot glas is dipped in liquid after being blown to create fissures. Once it cools fown, it is reheated and mouth blown to cover the fissures.

The process creates a rough looking texture similar to that of an alligator's skin. It is best used as pattern borders or backgrounds. Again, expect this type to be a lot pricier than machine-made glass. You may want to hold off using it until you are a lot more familiar with crafting stained glass.

- **Dichroic** – This type of glass is more commonly used in making jewelry. However, there are contemporary patterns that use it to make the design more interesting. Dichroic looks almost magical as it seems to change color as you move.

This color changing effect is a result of the layers of transparent metal oxides the glass is coated with. The coating enhances the light that passes through the glass creating dramatic changes in hues. Dichroic is quite expensive, but with the amazing lighting effect it produces, it is certainly worth every cent.

- **Drapery Glass** – As its name suggests, this glass type delivers a texture that looks like fabric drapes. It is perfect for designs that include clothing, which is why you often see it in cathedral or church windows. The stained glass designs depicting the saints and other religious themes make use of this type to make the robes more realistic.

However, despite how useful this texture may seem, it isn't a glass type that's used often by hobbyists. And this is because Drapery is a lot thicker than other types, so it is more difficult to cut and shape. So, while it may come in useful on some later projects, this isn't the type of glass that you may want to work with as a beginner.

- **English Muffle** - Originally produced by Wissmach Glass Company, this type of glass is perfect for traditional designs and patterns. It features a ripple texture that's non-directional. This means you can easily cut and shape the glass without having to worry about matching the pattern direction.

The English Muffle was traditionally used in Victorian windows so you'll see it quite often being utilized in restoration projects. However, because of the somewhat muted shades that this type comes in, it is also now quite popular in contemporary designs.

- **Gluechip** – The texture's name alone gives you an idea of how the surface design of this glass is created. Hot animal glue is applied to cold glass and allowed to dry it special humidity and temperature conditions. The glue contracts while it dries and chips off some of the glass. This produces a pattern that looks quite similar to whatyou would see on the window pane during cold winters. The beautiful frost-like pattern the glue creates makes this glass ideal as a border or background.

- **Seedy Glass** – The bubbles found in glass are also called seeds. And this is the identifying feature of this type of glass. Unlike in full antique where the seeds naturally happen through the mouth-blowing method, the bubbles in seedy are deliberately created.

The air bubbles are introduced to molten glass before the sheet is formed. This produces more seeds than what can be found in full antique. While it makes quite an attractive border and bakground option, seedy glass can be a bit tricky to cut.

- **Iridescent Glass** – While it is listed as a glass type, iridescent is more of a surface texture. It is characterized by the colorful shimmering effect it produces when light goes through or bounces on it. It is the obvious choice for designs that need an ethereal or whimsical look such as fairy or angelic images. You'll find that other types of glass can also have this surface treatment.

The glass types mentioned above are just some of the many options available. Some of the glasses are only available from specific manufacturers and cannot be bought at your local hardware store. You can check online stores or inquire from other stained glass hobbyists at online communties for the best places to get glass from.

2. **Glass Grinder** – This tool will come in quite handy as you work on your projects. When you purchase the glasses that you will be using, these come in panels that you need to reshape ad cut. And if you've ever

broken glass then you know just how dangerous those edges can be.

The grinder smoothens down the edges of the glass to prevent any accidents. This makes getting the right shape and size a lot easier as well. Glass grinder prices range from $60 to about $200. Don't forget to check reviews or talk to other folks who do stained glass to get recommendations about which grinder to purchase.

3. **Safety Glasses** – This is one tool that you certainly need to have. You'll be cutting, grinding and soldering glass so make sure that your eyes are protected. There are quite a lot of safety glasses available at you local hardware store. Pick the one that you're most comfortable in as you will be wearing it quite a lot. Also, make sure to ask the vendor if the pair you choose is suitable and can actually keep you safe from glass particles and shards. .

4. **Patterns** –Even the masters like Leonardo da Vinci and Micheal Angelo sketched their works of art before actually executing these on the canvas of their choice. So, don't think that you'd have to work on the glass directly immediately. To avoid wasting your materials, you would want to start with a pattern. As a beginner, you may want to use ready made patterns available online or from crafting books.

These designs have been tested and often rated based on difficulty.

5. **Basic Drafting Materials** – These materials include everything you need to be able to create your patterns such as pattern paper, tracing paper, metal ruler, pencils, markers and board papers. You can add any other supply that you may feel like you need to be able to prepare your design.

6. **Oil Glass Cutter** – As the name suggests, this tool is used to cut glass. There are a variety of cutter styles and brands available to choose from. It is recommended though that you get a pencil or comfort grip cutter. This type is more ideal for stained glass cutting as it is easier to hold. You may find a cheaper variety at your local hardware store, but these aren't always suitable for creating the shapes and forms you need.

7. **100- Watt Soldering Iron** – This tool give you the heat you need for your soldering needs. While a soldering gun may provide more voltage, stained glass crafting requires the flexibility that the iron brings. It is advisable that you choose quality over price when getting this tool as you will be using quite a lot.

8. **Flux and brush–** This is a chemical that you will need when you solder. It strips away the outer part of the copper foil so you can solder more efficiently. There are quite a few brands to choose from so it may get a bit overwhelming. Check the descriptions of the brand as well as the reviews from other hobbyists. You want flux that's odorless and smokeless such as Classic 100.

    Keep in mind that flux is acid so it needs to be handled very carefully. It can burn away on your clothes and even your skin so make sure you don't keep it lying around where it can be knocked over.Applying the flux can be tricky as well so you will need a brush to avoid accidents.

9. **Patina** – This is another chemical that you will need to have available. It is applied once you are done soldering and cleaning your copper foil project. It changes the color of the solder depending on the type of patina you use. If you use copper patina then the solder will turn into copper. If you apply black patina then that's the color the solder will turn into. Patina's average around $3.00 and can be easily purchased from craft stores.

10. **Copper Foil** – This tool is used to keep the glass pieces together. As a beginner, you may want to start with a 1/4 inch foil. You also want to make sure that you get

the plain copper foil instead of the ones that are silver or black back. You can opt for a different size and type once you become more used to working with the tool.

When you're more confident with your skill in stained glass crafting, you can follow the guide below on what size to use:

- 3/16 inch – Ideal for tapered or thin glass such as bevel. It will also work perfectly with smaller pieces.

- 7/32 inch – this is the most commonly used size as it works well with different types of glass. It also allows a thin edging that's not too excessive.

- ¼ inch – Perfect for heavier glass or when you want to double up the layers used.

- Full Sheet – Used for accents or as overlay

There are different brands of copper foil available to choose from. There are even some that come with scalloped edges for a more interesting and decorative look. You can check with other hobbyists or craftsmen on online communities to find the best one to work with. This will cost about $7-$8 dollars per roll depending on the brand.

11. **Scissors** – This is for cutting the foil to the size and form you need. You don't need to worry about having to get a special kind of shears as ordinary scissors will do just fine.

12. **Lead Came** – This is used for the same purpose as the copper foil. It is what keeps the pieces of the glass together so you can create your design. There are 2 types of came,

- H Shaped – used to hold 2 pieces of glass together

- U Shaped – used for borders

This material also comes in a variety of face shapes and sizes and strip lengths so it won't be difficult to find what you need for your project. So whether you need flat, rounded, wide or narrow strips, your local craft store should have it available.

13. **Fume Extractor/Smoke Absorber** – Over exposure to solder fumes is dangerous to your health. It can result in conditions such as asthma and other respiratory ailments. It has also been known to cause headaches and nosebleeds. So if you'll be working quite a lot on your stained glass projects, you will

need to have a fume extractor or smoke absorber to lessen the health risks. You can purchase one for as low as $50. The more high end absorber or extractor can set you back over $200.

14. **Fid or Burnishing Tool** – This tool is used to make sure that there are no gaps between the glass and the foil. What it does is help you press the foil more firmly onto the glass. If you don't have one, there are alternatives you can use instead. Chopsticks, the barrel of a pen or even a small wallpaper seam roller are great substitutes for this tool. Burnishing tools average about $6 at your local craft store.

15. **Running Pliers** - You'll need these pliers to break out your glass after these are scored. With this tool, you can break out practically any shape so you get the design or pattern that you want. As crafting tools go, running pliers are not cheap. They average around $10-$11 dollars.

16. **Cutting Oil** - This is used to keep your cutter lubricated while cutting glass. It can be used by feeding it in the oil well (if your cutter has one) or by dipping the wheel of your cutter while scoring. There are also other alternatives that you can use such as sewing machine oil or kerosene. The latter though has a strong odor that you may find overwhelming while working.

It is important to remember though that excessive oiling while scoring may affect the quality of your solder. It will make sticking the foil to the glass a lot harder, so use it sparsely if you will be using copper foil.

17. **Combination breaking-grozing pliers** – When creating your stained glass project, you will need both breaking and grozing pliers. This exonomical combination tool lets you get both for the price of one. This means you can easily break what you have scored and finish the glass without having to reach for another tool. This type of pliers averages around $10.

18. **Glass Grinder** – This tool helps you smoothen the edges of the pieces of glass that you cut. Both hobbyists and craftsmen find this an extremely useful tool to have around.

    When looking to purchase a grinder, you need to consider the following,

    - **Price** – grinders for home use can cost anywhere from under $100 to $370. The great thing about investing in this tool is that they are easy to resell should you choose to upgrade at a later time.

- **RPM** – this stands for rotations per minute. So basically, this is how fast the grinder head turns. The average is about 2850 to 3600. For more efficient grinding, choose one that has higher RPM.

- **Torque** – This feature describes the tool's resistance to glass. It is measured in inches to ounce. If you're going to be working on stained glass projects as a hobby then a torque of 20 should be fine. However, if you are looking to be more of a serious artist then 21-29 is the ideal choice. There are also torques that range above 29. These types are perfect for heavy duty projects.

- **Surface Size** – This is the table or the work area that's around the bit or head. Find a grinder that has a surface that you find comfortable in. Large tables are perfect if you'll be working with bigger pieces. However, it can get difficult to work on small details with that amount of space. There are grinders that have 2 tier surfaces that are quite popular among hobbyists and creaftsmen.

- **Manufacturer's Guarantee and Warranty** – As with most tools that you will be investing in, your grinder is certainly going to see a lot of action. This can lead to wear and tear. Parts replacement can prove to be costly, so check what the manufacturer's guarantee and warranty are.

- **Extra Features** – Despite serving the same basic function, not all grinders have been created equal. There are features in some that you may find useful such as sponge free cooling systems. It would be good to check at additional features and comparing which one works best for you before making your purchase.

Find out more about the best grinders by checking with other hobbyists stained glass artists on online communities. You can also visit the websites of manufacturers to get more information about the features their grinders have.

The tools listed above are just the basic ones you will need. There are other additional tools that more complex projects may require. But as a beginner, you can stick to what's listed here until you become more confident with the techniques and start working on more complicated crafts.

In addition to the tools, it is also important that you know some basic concepts and methods involved in the projects.

Foil versus Lead

Constructing your stained glass project is very similar to completing a jigsaw puzzle. You have different pieces that you need to fit together to create the design you want. An essential part of the craft is sticking the pieces together so they form a whole.

There are 2 different methods to choose from, copper foiling and lead came. There has been much debate on which of the two is the best. Some folks say that copper foiling is easier and more flexible while others prefer using lead.

Each method has its own benefits. Below is a guide to help you better understand which to choose:

1. **Copper Foiling** – this method involves wrapping the foil around the glass and leaving a thin overlay on the edge. It is ideal for the following conditions,

- a. Projects where lateral strength and rigidity is essential.
- b. 3 dimesional projects such as boxes or shades for lamps.
- c. Small projects where there aren't a lot of pieces involved in the construction.
- d. Lightweight projects

2. **Lead Came** – This method involves attaching a strip of came to the edge of the glass. It is ideal for the following conditions,
    - a. Projects with geometrical patterns
    - b. Projects that will be exposed to the elements

There are no strict rules as to which method should be used. It all depends on personal preference. However, the conditions mentioned above are from hobbyists and craftsmen whose recommendations are based on their own experience.

Chapter 2- The Process

There are numerous processes involved in creating a stained glass project. Whether you're working on a window or a suncatcher, the steps are basically the same.

You can use the glossary guide below to help you understand the different steps included in the process.

Term	Definition/Description
Template	Pattern made from either cardboard or paper that's used as a guide to create the glass pieces
Leadline	The outlines of the of the forms or shapes for patterns that the glass will be cut into
Grain Direction	The orientation of the glass' texture
Cartoon	A 2D rendition of the design done in full scale
Scoring	Creating a break in the glass with the cutter to make it easier to break into the needed shapes

Working piece	A piece or segment that you will be using while working. For example, a working piece of glass is a small cut from the larger sheet. A working piece of solder is a specific length cut instead of using the entire roll
burnish	The process of folding and pressing down on the foil so that it adheres to all the surfaces of the glass.
Jig	A frame used to hold the glass pieces in place
Leading	The process of applying lead came to the glass pieces
Joins	The point where 2 lead came meet to keep 2 or more pieces of glasses together

Step 1: Choosing the Pattern

When crafting stained glass, the first thing you need to do is to choose a design or pattern. There are hundreds of free patterns available online, at crafting stores and in books that you can use. The great thing about working with designs that have already been used by others is that pretty much everything has already been figured out. From the type of glass to be used to the shapes of the pieces needed, all the information you need is available.

As a beginner, you can use these free patterns to get used to the intricacies of the craft such as what shapes and forms are easy to transfer on to glass. Once you become more competent with the cutting and other processes you can start working on your own unique patterns.

You also want to consider choosing simple patterns for your first few projects. This will help you practice the different skills such as cutting and soldering without getting overwhelmed. These basic patterns will also ensure that you finish the first few stained glass projects that you work on.

If you create your own pattern, you can begin by sketching what the design will look like on a smaller scale. This part will help you determine the different elements that will go into the pattern prior to making the templates.

Step 2: Creating the Template

Once you have selected the design you want to use, it's time to create your template.

Follow the procedure below:

1. Prepare the following tools and materials

    a. Graph Paper

    b. Permanent Marker

    c. Scissors

    d. Pens

    e. Ruler

2. Draw or trace the pattern onto the graph paper. You can also choose to print out the

pattern if you don't feel confident about doing it freehand. It is important that you use graph paper as it makes it easier to keep the details in proportion.

Make sure that the leadlines do not stop in space as this will create problems when you assemble the glass pieces that will be cut using the template. It is also important to put a leadline from the points acute and right angles.

The thickness or tip width of the marker you use to draw the leadlines will also have an effect on the final product. So, if you use a thicker marker, make sure to consider that as the allowance.

3. Cut out the pieces of the pattern. Make sure to label each with the color and grain direction to avoid confusion later on.

Step 3: Scoring and Cutting the Glass

When you have the template ready, you can now start working with your glass.

1. Select the glass types you will be using for each piece. If you will be using different textures, it is important to make sure that all the glass types have the same thickness. Unless you want some pieces to appear embossed, a uniform thickness will ensure that your stained glass' surface is flat and somewhat smooth.

2. Gather the materials you need including the following:

   a. Template pieces
   b. Glass Cutter
   c. Cutting Oil

d. Goggles
   e. gloves

3. Cover your workspace with sheets of newspaper to help catch the shards of glass as well as protect the table you are using. You can put numerous sheets so you can easily remove the sheet on top when it gets small slivers.

4. Place the paper template under the glass (or above for opaque glass) you will be using and trace the design using a permanent marker. Make sure to leave about a centimeter on the border for the foil. If you cut the glass to the exact size of the template without an allowance, it may be difficult to assemble the pieces once the foils or came are attached.

5. If your cutter has an oil well, fill it with the cutting oil to protect your tool and to make nicer cuts on the glass. If it doesn't have a well, you can dab some oil on it instead. Make sure you don't over lubricate as this may have an impact on your soldering later on.

   a. Standing up while scoring and cutting your glass will help you control your cutter better. So, if you are able to, this is the recommended position for this step.

b. Wear safety goggles and gloves at all time when scoring and cutting. Glass can be dangerous to work with so you want to make sure you are protected at all times.

c. You can choose to either push or pull the cutter depending on which motion you are more comfortable with. You'll find that some shapes or forms are easier to cut with pushing while others work better with pulling.

d. Make sure that the cutter is perpendicular to the glass during the entire process. It is important to maintain this position even if you are working on curved lines. If the cutter leans to the sides then the sharp edges of your tool will not be properly touching the glass thus affecting the cut.

e. Ensure that you are able to see the lines you are following as well as the cutter wheel while scoring and cutting.

f. Maintain equal pressure throughout the entire cut. If you let up on certain sections, the score will not be even. This will make breaking the glass much difficult and may also result in uneven breaks.

g. Watch the amount of pressure that you apply when scoring and cutting. Pressing too hard may damage your wheel as well as the glass you are working on. It also puts too much strain on your hand and shoulder and you'll end up feeling sore before you get everything done.

h. It is best to start cutting about a sixteenth of an inch (1/16") from the edge of the glass and roll your cutter over until you get to the other side. Be careful that you don't end up jamming your tool onto your worktable.

i. When following the lines you drew using your template, it is essential that you cut on the inside. Cutting on the outer edge of the line may result in your glass pieces being bigger than what you need. That will certainly make fitting these all together much harder later on.

j. Regardless of how big your workspace is, it is always better to use a working piece rather than the entire glass sheet. Smaller pieces will be easier to handle so you can move the glass around while cutting and scoring.

k. If one of the shapes has a deep curve, it is best to do it in small cuts rather than completing it in one swipe. You should also cut it towards the middle part of your glass. Having the mass around it (further from the edge) will prevent fractures and breakage,

l. Don't leave the most difficult cut for last. It is advisable to get the harder shapes cut first.

Once you have scored and cut your glass properly, it will be easy to break off the pieces you need. You can follow the methods below,

- For curved pieces, you can continue using your cutter until you separate the needed shape from your working piece.

- For straight pieces, you can hold the glass and snap it apart or use a pair of pliers. Just place the pliers on the crack and the glass will separate once you squeeze the tool.

There's no need to worry if you get some jagged edges. You can easily fix that on the next step.

Step 4: Grinding the Edges

No matter how experienced you get, there are bound to be some uneven edges on the glass pieces you cut. Grinding will smoothen out the vertical edges so that the pieces can fit together properly. For this step, it is ideal to have 2 types of grinding head.

For the pieces with straight edges, a wider grinding head is recommended. You can use one with a ¾" diameter to take care of this. A smaller or ¼" diameter head on the other hand is perfect for the intricate curves.

When mounting or positioning your grinder, consider what position you will be most comfortable in. If you will be doing it standing up, the grinder should be at a height where you can bend your arms while managing the glass. Any lower or higher and you'll end up straining your arms, shoulders and lower back.

Some folks find putting a foot up on a stool while grinding helps in maintaining proper balance. Try this if you will be grinding glass while standing up.

Here are some tips to keep in mind when grinding:

a. Make sure to wear your safety goggles to protect your eyes from dust and shards of glass.

b. The jagged edges on the glass pieces can be dangerous. To avoid getting cut, wrap surgical tape around your fingers before putting your gloves on for extra protection.

c. Check the water reservoir of your grinder. Make sure that it is in the right level as this is crucial when you begin grinding.

d. To prevent your glass pieces from getting water damaged, cover the surfaces with laminated plastic.

e. Make sure to have your templates ready and within reach so you can check the glass pieces during the grinding process.

f. Keep a towel in hand. You'll need to dry off the pieces before you set them against your paper template.

g. Put a splash guard around your grinder. Since there will be water involved in the process, there's likely to be some splattering.

h. Check the lighting in your work area first. When grinding glass, you'll need 2 sources of light to be able to see clearly. You should have sufficient overhead lighting. To compensate for the shadow your upper body will create, you also want to make sure you have a light in front of you.

i. Each type of glass grinds differently. So, before grinding the pieces you'd cut out, practice with scraps first to see how that type grinds. This will certainly save you a lot of time and money as you won't end up damaging the pieces you need.

j. For deep cuts or curves, it is best to push the piece in the opposite direction. If your grinder is like most available models, the head should rotate in a counter clockwise direction. Position your glass and push it in a clockwise direction to get to the deeper curves.

k. For shallower curves, you can position your glass and push it in the same direction as the grinder head is moving.

l. While grinding, keep an eye on the water reservoir and the sponge. Make sure the reservoir has enough water all the time. The sponge should also always be wet when grinding glass.

Glass grinders are an essential tool in crafting stained glass. There are those who prefer working with a sickle stone but this can get pretty tedious. However, if you find this method more up your alley then you can use it instead.

When you are done grinding the edges of your pieces, it is best that you assemble your pattern to check if the pieces all fit together. You can create a jig or a temporary frame to keep everything in place. You can also use push pins on the perimeter side if you don't have materials for a jig.

Step 5: Applying Copper Foil or Lead Came

To get the pieces to stick to each other you will need to apply either foil or came to the edges of the glass. As mentioned in a previous chapter, certain projects work better with each method. You can use the guide provided previously to choose which one to utilize.

Applying the foil or the came is an integral part of the process as it affects the next step, which is soldering. If improperly done, it will be difficult to get the pieces adhered to each other. Below are the procedures for each method.

Copper Foiling

This is the process of applying a continuous strip of copper foil on the edges of the glass. This is done so pieces can be adhered to each other through soldering later on. Solder does not stick on glass, hence the need for the foil.

1. Clean the edges of your glass. Whether you used a grinder, a sickle stone or any other method, your glass will need to be cleaned to make sure the foil sticks to it better. You can do this by wiping it with rubbing

alcohol. This will remove dust, oil, and whatever other residue there may be on the glass piece.

2. Choose the foil you will be using. As described in an earlier chapter, there are a variety of widths that you can choose from.

3. Gather the rest of your tools together.

    a. Knife (exacto)

    b. Roller or fid

    c. Scissors

    d. Pencil or pen or thin dowel

4. Take the glass you will be foiling. To ensure the quality of foiling, you'll need to do one piece at a time.

5. Hold the glass between your thumb and middle fingers with the edge you will be foiling at the bottom.

6. Take your foil and hold it with the paper backing on top and the non-adhesive side at the bottom. Peel off about an inch or two of the paper and center the glass edge on it. Make sure that there's equal foil width on either side.

7. Do not start at the edge of the piece or on an external side (the side that will be part

of the perimeter of the stained glass project)

8. Press down firmly on the foil to make it stick to the edge of the glass. Push the glass away from you while peeling more of the backing paper away.

9. For deep curves, it is best that you apply the foil a little at a time. Easing it in will prevent the copper foil from tearing. Make sure that you press it to the edge gently and regularly check that it isn't stretched too tightly. You don't want it splitting later on.

10. Once you get to the point where you began and end by overlapping about a sixteenth of an inch. Check if the overlap is straight and parallel to the layer underneath.

11. Take your fid (or chopsticks or pen) and roll it over the foil covered edges. Apply a little pressure to make the foil stick to the edges more securely.

12. With the foil applied, it is now time to crimp the foil. This is basically folding the foil onto the top and bottom of the glass with your thumb and index finger. Pinch the two sides of the foil until it presses down on the surface and the bottom. Make sure that the copper foil is even on both sides. If it isn't, you will need to refoil.

This will require a bit of hand and eye coordination so you may want to practice beforehand on a scrap piece of glass. There are also tools such as crimpers that can make the job easier.

13. For corners, avoid bunching up the foil. Instead, tuck it on one side first before folding it down on the other.

14. Trim the uneven foil on the overlap with a cutter.

15. When you're done crimping, burnish the foil with your fid or alternative tool. This will ensure that it is stuck securely on the glass to avoid flux from seeping in later. Take care that you don't rip or tear any of the foil while burnishing.

Remember that solder will not stick to glass. So, the better you wrap it with foil, the better the adhesion to the other pieces will be. It's also best not to leave foiled glasses lying around for an extended time. The copper foil may oxidize and will not be able to accept solder.

Lead Came

Lead came is the traditional method used in stained glass. It is best for panels that will be exposed to the elements. Before you start working with this material it is important that you remember the following,

- Do not eat while handling lead came. While most came materials now are not fully made of just lead, the amount of lead in it is still dangerous to your health.

- Wash your hands after handling lead came.

Leading can be tricky so you may want to practice with scraps pieces of glass before working on your actual project. But the more you get used to the technique you'll find that it will be a lot easier to do.

1. Prepare the tools and materials that you need,

    a. Glass pieces (cut and grinded)

    b. Nails (horseshoe)

    c. Lead clippers/lead knife

    d. Lead came

    e. Lead stretcher (vise)

    f. Pliers

    g. Straight wooden batons (4 pieces)

    h. Chipboard(about 3 inches bigger than your pattern)

    i. Fid

    j. Nails(regular)

    k. Set square

    l. hammer

2. Lead came comes in both spools and 6 foot length bars. These can be round or flat and in different widths. Regardless of being made from the same materials you'll find that some came are soft and pliant while others are much harder. As a beginner you want to get the former as the latter can be harder to cut.

3. The first thing you need to do before attaching the lead to your glass pieces is to stretch and strengthen it. This will make the came more rigid and less floppy as when you first get it.

    a. Attach one end of the came to a vise.

    b. Take pliers to hold the other end of the came

    c. Standing with a solid stance (one leg slightly in front) pull on the came by tugging on the pliers. Keep doing sharp little tugs until you feel it cannot be stretched anymore. Be careful though as pulling too much may break the lead.

d. Lay the stretched lead on the table and run your fid through the channel. This will open it up and make it easier for you to fit in your glass piece and putty later on.

4. Take your template (paper pattern) and lay it against your prepared piece of board. This will serve as the backing of your jig.

5. Take the wooden batons and create your jig. Make sure to leave enough space between the end of the template and the batons. This allowance is for the perimeter leading.

6. The first came you will be preparing are the ones for the border or perimeter. Take the came and measure it into the space you'd left earlier.

   If there are angles on the perimeter, you need to create these before cutting the border lead.

    a. Take the piece of came for the angle and place it where it's supposed to be. With a pen or your lead knife, mark the top part of the came. This will serve as a guide for cutting.

    b. Take your lead nippers and cut through the marked line on the came.

7. With the border lead done, you can start working on the glass pieces. It is best to use a ¼" or a 3/16" came. If you use something thicker, it may end up overshadowing the glass. You can use different widths to highlight certain sections of your project.

8. Stretch the came you will be using for the pieces as you did with the ones used for the

border. Open up the channels so the glass can be slipped in.

9. Remember to cut the came a bit shorter than the glass piece to make allowance for the other came strip it will be butting against.

10. Long thin angles can be a challenge to lead. You can use your lead knife positioned at a flat angle to push the lead slightly to the angle you need it at.

11. Continue to apply the lead came to the other glass panels.

12. With more lead on your project, you may find that it can get more difficult to keep in place. You can use horseshoe nails and

scrap lead to keep everything where they're supposed to be.

13. Add the glass pieces in a diagonal direction starting on the left hand top side if you are right handed and on the opposite side if you are left handed.

14. Don't forget to keep checking your template to see if you are sticking to the pattern. If your panel seems like it's getting bigger, you can disassemble what you've made to check where it needs to be fixed. With the lead already cut, it will be a lot easier to put back together than when you first started leading the pieces.

    If the glass has been cut properly and grinded to the right size and shape, chances are, it's the lead that needs to be trimmed.

15. When you finish leading the glass panels, it's time to work on the remaining borders. Start with the vertical edge. Lay the lead came on the edge to see how much you will need. Measure the right length, mark and then cut. Don't forget to leave room for the lead you will be using for the horizontal one.

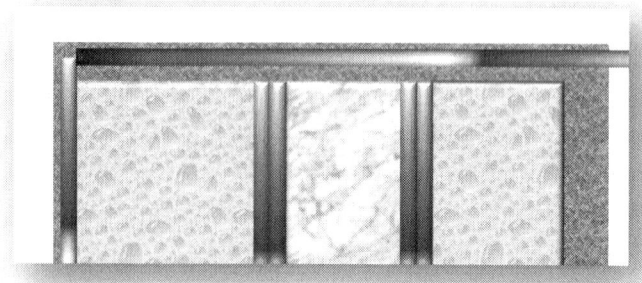

16. Lay the lead came on the remaining side and repeat the procedure in the previous step.

17. Take the 2 remaining batons and place them on the remaining open side of your jig. Use a set square to ensure they are at the right angles before nailing them down.

After foiling or leading, your panel or project is now ready for soldering.

Step 6: Soldering

The next step in the process is to solder your glass pieces together. Below are the procedures to follow for both copper foiling and lead came:

Soldering Foil

1. Gather the tools and materials you will be using,

    a. Liquid flux

    b. Flux applicator or Q tips

    c. 60/40 solder

d. 100 watt iron (80 watt can also be used)

e. Dry paper towels

f. Wet paper towels or sponge

g. Fume extractor

2. Before soldering, you need to make sure that you have enough ventilation in the room. You can also set up your fume extractor. Check the manufacturer's instruction to make sure this is done properly. There will be quite a lot of fumes during this process, so make sure that you are protected.

3. Take your soldering iron and plug it in. You need a really hot iron so be careful that you don't burn yourself.

4. Put a wet sponge or paper towel within reach. You will need this to periodically wipe of the tip of your iron to keep it clean.

5. Take your liquid flux and applicator. Take the pieces you will be working on and apply flux on the foil. The amount of flux is crucial. Make sure you don't over or under flux the foil. Apply just enough to see a wet coat on the foil without it looking like it is dripping.

6. As a beginner, you may find it difficult to hold the entire roll of solder in your hand.

To address this, cut working pieces that's about five to six rolls on your hand. Prepare a few of these working pieces so you don't have to pause when you run out of solder.

7. If your panel or project is not in a jig or frame, hold the pieces in place with push pins or tacks.

8. Choose the seam you will be working on.

9. Take your iron and touch it to the seam you will be working on.

10. Touch the tip of the solder on the top of the iron and push gently.

11. Work your iron down the seam while pressing down on the solder. Keep moving in a continuous motion and avoid stopping in the middle of the seam. Watch the amount of solder that's being applied. The goal is to have a rounded bead on the seam. If there isn't enough solder, you won't get what you are aiming for. Too much solder on the other hand will look to heavy.

12. If you are working towards the edge, lift the solder off the iron when you are about 2 inches away. You should have enough left over solder to cover that area.

13. If it's your first time soldering, it's okay to pause after each seam to check if there's

any spot you need to touch up. You can use the method below:

    a. Touch your iron to the area that needs to be touched up.

    b. Push down until your iron touches glass.

    c. Allow the solder on both sides to melt.

    d. Lift the iron up and the melted solder will settle in a smoother bead

14. Continue soldering until all of the seams are done.

15. Wipe the surface with a dry paper towel.

16. Turn over the panel or project and solder the opposite side. When done, wipe it with a dry paper towel as you did on the other side.

17. Fix any spots that need touching up.

18. Set your panel with the right side up. You will now be soldering the edge of your project.

19. Hold your iron so that it is facing outward. Your hand and the solder should be above the panel. This is to ensure that the solder will not just drip down the edge without settling on the glass edge.

20. Apply the solder with the iron around the perimeter on the top surface. If you will be using your hand to turn your project, make sure that you are wearing protective gloves as hot solder can be extremely painful if you accidentally touch it.

21. Wipe the surface with a dry paper towel when you are done.

22. Turn the panel or project over and do the same thing for the edge on the bottom surface.

23. Wipe the surface with a dry towel.

24. The last part you need to solder is the glass edge. Hold your panel so that the edge you will be soldering is facing up.

25. Flux the edge and do a touch and lift motion (the method used to touch up seams) until you have all edges soldered. You should have enough solder from the top and bottom perimeter soldering to cover the edge. You can add some more solder if needed.

Soldering Lead Came

The process for soldering panels assembled with lead came is different from the process used in copper foiling. Since the panels are already held together by the came, you only need to work on the joints. Below are the steps you need to follow:

1. Gather your materials together. Make sure you have the following prepared,

    a. Soldering iron

    b. 50/50 solder

    c. Flux and applicator

    d. Damp flannel for cleaning

    e. Wire brush

2. Turn your iron on. It may take a while to get hot enough, so you want to make sure you give it enough time before using it.

3. Take your wire brush and clean up the joins and surface of your panel.

4. Make sure that your area is well ventilated. You can get a fume extractor to deal with the fumes.

5. Apply flux to the joins that you will be soldering.

6. Cut off short sticks of solder.

7. When your iron is hot enough, take your solder and touch the tip to the join you will be working on. Touch your hot iron to the solder and let a melted drop settle on the join. It's okay to add a little solder at a time as it can be quite impossible to remove it from lead.

8. Hold the iron and solder in place until you see a nice round solder bead on the join. Be careful not to touch the lead with the iron. While it does need to get heated up as well, let the solder do it to prevent it from melting too much.

   Also, holding the iron steady will also ensure that the solder will not look messy or rough. Patience goes a long way when you're soldering lead.

9. Solder all the joins.

10. Wait for the solder to cool down before proceeding.

11. When your panel is ready, lift it up carefully and turn it on the other side. Your panel will be quite fragile at this point, so make sure you handle it gently.

12. While supporting the panel with your hand, brush the joins at the bottom to prepare it for soldering.

13. Follow the same steps you did when soldering the front of the panel.

14. When the solder has cooled down on both sides, clean the joins and the came from excess flux with your wire brush.

Solder is the glue that holds your pieces together. After you're done soldering, you should be able to enjoy the design of your pattern. However, it will still look quite rough. The next step will help it look a lot nicer.

Step 7: Finishing

Your panel is almost ready to be displayed. All you need now are the finishing touches. This involves cleaning, polishing and applying patina (optional) to make your project look even more incredible.

Cleaning

1. After soldering, you need to wash your stained glass panel. If done properly, it will neutralize the flux you've applied earlier.
2. Gather the following ingredients for the best results,
    a. Sudsy ammonia all purpose cleaner. These can be store bought or you can make your own with the following recipe:

- You will need a spray bottle. You can buy new ones as these are inexpensive anyways. Using old ones that had been filled with other cleaners may leave a chemical residue despite being cleaned. Choose a bottle that can hold about 12 ounces.

- Fill it about ¾ with water

- Pour ammonia in the water until it fills the remaining space. Leave some more room for the other ingredients though.

- Add about a teaspoon of dishwashing liquid.

- Add a quart (or less) of rubbing alcohol.

- Close the bottle and shake gently.

b. Wax Cleaner – You can get this at practically any car care center around the country. They come in different brands but Mother's Wax has been recommended by experts.

c. Industrial Scrub Pads

    d. Paper Towels – Cloth towels don't dry glass as efficiently as paper towels. So, make sure you use this.

    e. Patina

3. Pour some of your ammonia cleaner on the panel (or project) and start scrubbing until you see suds. Make sure to scrub on the solder lines as well. Wash both the top and bottom surfaces. Be careful that you don't drop the panel as it can get quite slippery at this point.

4. Use the paper towels to dry the panel completely.

5. Take your wax cleaner and apply it to the panel, both the glass and solder lines. Buff off the wax with a cloth or paper towel until no more black rubs off. That black substance is produced from oxidation. If you don't remove this, it will react with the patina and the result will not be pretty. You can stop at this point if you wish your panel to have a silver finish. Some extra waxing is all you'll need.

Applying Patina

Patina changes the color a metal's outer layer. Applying it to your panel will give the solder lines a more finished look.

1. **Copper Patina** – This gives your panel a bronze look that can look quite stunning. Below are the procedures applying this type of patina:

    a. If you're applying the patina on a copper foiled panel, make sure that you are using one that is made for solder. If it's made for lead or zinc, the effect will be quite different.

    b. Pour some of it directly to your panel. Spread it out using your scrubbing pad or cloth. Make sure that the cloth or pad you are using is dry.

c. Wipe any excess patina with dry paper towels.

d. Do steps b and c for the bottom part of your panel as well.

e. Leave it propped up for air drying. Make sure that it is well supported to avoid any accidents.

f. When the patina has dried, apply some wax to the panel. Leave it to dry before buffing and polishing. If there are any wax stuck on the corners or the solder lines, take a dry toothbrush to clean that off.

2. **Black Patina** – This gives the solder lines a darker tint.

a. Pour out some in a container and mix in a teaspoon of salt or vinegar to enhance the color. Do not pour back this mixture to the rest of the patina if there are any left over.

b. If you're applying it to a panel with copper foil, pour the patina mixture on the panel and spread it with your scrubbing pad. Once the solder lines are black, rinse the patina off with water.

c. If you're applying it to a lead panel, dip a brush or Q tip into the patina mixture and apply it to the came and solder.

d. Pat it dry with paper towels and leave to air dry overnight or for 24 hours.

e. When the panel is dry, apply wax and let it dry before buffing and polishing

As a beginner, following the steps in this chapter may seem challenging at first. Remember that stained glass crafting can be tricky and it may take a while for you to master all the techniques. Be patient and make time to practice the different steps with scraps before working on your actual panel.

Chapter 3 –Stained Glass – Painting

There is another stained glass technique that doesn't involve much glass cutting, foiling, leading or even soldering. It is also commonly known as faux stained glass. However, this method has been popular among craftsmen since the gothic period. This technique lets you become more creative as your design or pattern is not limited to what shape glass can be cut into.

Tools and Materials:

Stained Glass through painting is only limited by your imagination. Even if you're not much good at drawing, you can still create stunning stained glass pieces. Below are the tools and materials that you need to be able to create this work of art:

1. **Glass Paint** – also called enamels, this type of paint is a mixture of flux, metallic oxide pigments and ground glass. These are applied on the surface of glass decoration made permanent through firing on a kiln.

   While there are a lot of different kinds of glass paints, these can all be categorized into 2 main types,

   - Opaque – paint where only a minimal amount of light can pass through. This basically means that one cannot see through this paint. These come in 2 different subtypes:

     o Pigments – darker shades that include various hues such as black, brown, and grey. These are often used to highlight elements in the design. For example, stained glass windows depicting saints at churches often make use of pigment paint for the facial features.

- Color Paints – There are numerous color paints available in the market. Each manufacturer features their own tints so you can practically own dozens of yellows with each one in a different shade than the rest.

  This type of paint is best used when you want to have privacy in the room where the window or panel will be placed. It works best when the light source is on the front.

- Transparent – paint where light can pass through so one can easily see what's on the other side. This type comes in a wide range of colors. While it doesn't create the same impact as actual colored or textured glass, it does allow you to be more flexible. You don't have to worry about the shapes of your pattern being too hard to cut into glass.

2. **Stained –glass painting media** – When you get glass paint it is dry or in powder form. Before you can apply it with a brush and use it to paint your pattern,

you will need to dissolve it. The basic medium used (and ideal for beginners) is water.

3. **Gum Arabic** – This comes in both powder and liquid form. It is mixed in with the paint to strengthen the glass for firing in a kiln.

4. **Lightbox** – This is basically your workspace. It is ideally about 22"x16" or larger and made from strong glass. It is lit by a movable and low heat lighting source. What it does is give you an impression of what your design will look like with light hitting it or passing through it while you are working. You can have one custom made to fit the specifications you need.

However, if you do not have one, you can start off with a white oil cloth covered table. The cloth will simulate the white background produced by the lightbox.

5. **Stained glass painting palettes** – Used to mix and blend your paints. Opt for toughened or thicker glass about 8"x14".

6. **Paint Cover**- Regardless of how dedicated you are to your project, chances are you won't be able to complete the painting in just one session. The last thing you want to happen is to waste any of the glass paint you have already mixed on your

palette. After all, glass paints such as Reusche can be expensive.

To keep your paint safe from dust, you can use glazed porcelain ramekins for cooking and baking. This will certainly keep your paint free from any impurities in between sessions.

7. **Brushes** – Since you will be doing quite a lot of painting, you will of course need to have brushes on hand. Below are the types that you will need:

   a. **Wide Narrow Brushes** – This is used for applying the under and overcoat on your work of art.

   b. **Large Badger Blender** – This type definitely does not come cheap but with proper care, it can last for quite a long time. The purpose of this brush is to let you add texture to your work. It moves the paint around and blends the colors as well.

   c. **Tracing Brushes** – This much narrower type is used to create the lines in your design. You can choose either synthetic or natural brushes depending on what fits in your budget and your own personal preference. For natural brushes it is recommended though that you use sable as it works well with almost all mediums.

As a beginner, start off with 3 different sizes to take care of the different line thickness. Get a '6' for thicker lines and a '0' for the more delicate and fine strokes. For the mid size a '2' will do nicely.

8. **Palette Knife** – This tool is used to ground and mix your paint. Pick one between 6" – 8". These can be quite sharp so be careful with handling your knives.

9. **Painting Bridge** – Whether you are new to painting or quite experienced, your hands and wrist are bound to get unsteady now and then. A bridge helps prevent this from happening. It allows you to rest your arm while working so you have more control and less unsteady motions.

10. **Needles/Sticks** – These tools allow you to add more texture to your pattern. You can use virtually anything you want from chopsticks to knitting needles. You can experiment with what kind of pattern or texture a stick or needle creates prior to using these on your actual work.

11. **Jars (mason/jam)** – You'll need this to hold a number or materials and tools such as water, silver stain and your brushes.

12. **Scrubs** – This will be used to clean up your panels

13. **Kiln Trays**- Your panel will need to be fired to fire up the paint to make it adhere better to the glass. Some folks use kiln paper or wash but you can forego this. You can use calcium carbonate or whiting instead as a separator or to keep your panel from the tray.

14. **Kiln** – This allows the paint you'd applied on the surface to fuse to the glass.

15. **Mask** – Most glass paint contain lead. Inhaling this can be dangerous to your health. Ensure you are protected by wearing a mask.

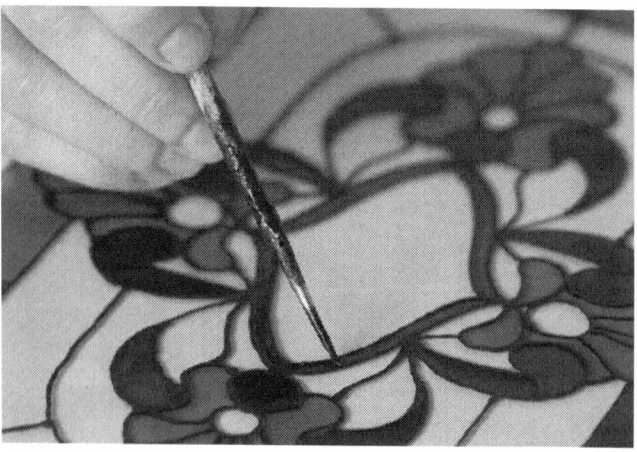

Making Stained Glass – Painting

Since the middle ages, artisans have been creating stunning painted stained glass for churches, businesses and homes. The intricate details produced by painting are something that cannot be produced by the cutting and assembling glass method.

Below is the process of how you too can create your own glass painting,

Step 1- Cleaning the Glass

Before you do anything else, the first step is to make sure that the glass you will be painting on is clean. Simply wiping it with a cloth or paper towel is not enough. If you want to avoid your paint beading up or not spreading the way you need it to, you will need to make sure your glass is cleaned properly,

You will need the following:

- Calcium carbonate or whiting
- Ammonia based window cleaner
- Dishwashing liquid soap
- Moist rag
- Dry rag

To clean your glass, follow the procedure below:

1. Take your moist rag and dip it in calcium carbonate or whiting

2. Scrub your glass for a few minutes. Make sure to scrub the entire surface to avoid any issues with the paint later on.

3. Wash off the whiting with dishwashing liquid

4. Apply ammonia based window cleaner and then wipe dry.

It is essential that you do not substitute the cleaning materials given in this section. Other cleaners such as acetone ad alcohol will not clean the glass as effectively.

Step 2: Creating the Outline

When you draw or paint something, you often start with the outline. This is the same with stained glass painting. The first step in your work of art is tracing the outline of your design. These are basically the black lines in the drawing that you will be filling out with color. When you are done, it should look something like a coloring book prior to the colors.

There are 2 different ways for you to create the outline. The first method which is with liquid lead is a lot easier to manage for a beginner. The second method or tracing back is something that you can try your hand on as soon as you are more comfortable holding and working with a brush.

Liquid Lead

For this method you will need the following,

- Liquid Lead – You can find these in both bottles and tubes at arts and crafts stores.

- Painting knife

- Marker (optional)

- Pattern (design)

- Clean glass

- Painting Bridge

Once all the materials are ready, you can follow the procedure below:

1. Print or draw the design you want to full size (the exact size of the design as you want it to appear).

2. Place the design underneath your working piece of glass.

3. Trace the design or the pattern with the marker or the liquid lead directly.

4. Don't forget to set up your painting bridge so you don't accidentally touch any wet liquid lead. This can cause a smudge a delay your project. If you do not have a bridge, then it is advisable that you start working on the top left hand corner and work your way down in a diagonal pattern if you are right handed. If you are right handed then do it from the top right hand side instead.

5. If you make a mistake with tracing the outline, do not wipe off the lead. Wait for it to dry and then scrape it off with your knife.

6. Once you have completed the outline, leave the lead to dry for at least 2 hours.

Tracing Black

You will need the following,

- Clean Glass
- Script Liner Brush – this is a thin brush that comes with longer hair. A size 1 or 2 will be ideal for this step.
- A painting knife
- A painting palette

- Water (or whatever medium your paint needs)
- Gum Arabic
- Lightbox
- Pointy stick

When you have all your tools and materials prepared, follow the steps below,

1. **Mix your paint on your glass painting palette**

    a. Pour the glass paint out

    b. Add the medium you need

    c. Sprinkle in some gum Arabic

    d. Mix with your painting knife until all the ingredients are well blended.

2. **Apply the paint on your glass**

    a. Place your working piece of glass on top of the lightbox

    b. Dip your brush into the paint.

    c. Draw the lines you need. Make sure that these are thick enough that it blocks the light coming from your lightbox underneath. Take care though that your lines don't appear lumpy.

d. Draw each section at a time to avoid accidentally touching dry paint with your brush later on.

e. Don't feel discouraged if the result looks more like an ink blot and less like your design.

3. **Scratch off excess paint**

a. Take your pointy stick (or a paintbrush bottom with the tip sharpened) and scratch out any paint that you don't need.

b. Create the angles and shapes more accurately by removing the excess paint.

c. This step can be quite tricky but extremely important. So, avoid rushing through it and take your time to clean off the paint.

4. **Fire your glass**

a. To make sure your tracing black fuses with the surface of your glass, you need to place it in a kiln.

b. Remember that opalescent or opaque and transparent glass needs different temperatures to fuse properly.

Step 3A: Filling in with Color

When the liquid lead has dried or after the tracing lines have been fused, you are now ready to add color to your panel. To do this, you will need the following,

- Glass paint
- Glass paint media such as water or thinner
- Glass paint palette
- Paint brushes
- Glass paint knife

As soon as you have your tools and materials ready, follow the procedure below,

1. Take your paint and pour it out onto your palette.
2. Add the medium and mix until you the powder paint is well dissolved.
3. Dip your brush into the paint
4. Paint or fill in the section of the panel with the appropriate colors.

5. Remember to wash your brush thoroughly before using it for a different color. It would be best if you have a separate brush for each tint if possible. Once the paint dries, you are all set to go.

Step 3B: Matting

Another technique you will need to know is matting. This gives your pattern a 3D effect similar to that of decorative windows that you often see displayed at churches. The procedure is different from what is described in step 3A.

You will need the following,

- Brushes
    - Badger
    - Arious 'scrubs'
    - Ox hair 'mop (1.5")
    - Other bristle brushes
- Light box
- Clean glass
- Stained glass palette
- Stained glass palette knife
- Glass paint
- Water
- Gum Arabica
- Pipette
- Lightbox

This technique works with tracing black and will not have the same effect if used with liquid lead. So, once after the tracing has been fired, you can follow the procedure below,

1. Mix your paint on the palette. The consistency should be similar to that of

evaporated milk. If you need to add water to your mixture, do not pour it directly. Instead dip your mop brush into water and then use it to dilute your paint.

2. Test the paint on a scrap piece of glass or on your lightbox before applying it to your project.

3. Take your mop brush and dip it into the paint.

4. Apply the paint on the entire surface in sweeping motions. With your mop at a 45degree angle, coat the glass with paint by brushing across from edge to edge.

5. Blend the matte paint with your badger by lightly brushing on the surface in figure 8 strokes.

6. If you want to add texture to the matt, you can stipple the surface. This is done by holding your badger at a 90-degree angle and tap in a staccato motion on the paint. This will produce little pinpricks of light.

7. Remove the paint in the areas outside of your pattern when it dries. You can do that with a bristle brush. If you used sufficient amount of Gum Arabica then it should be easy to do.

8. Use your different bristle brushes to create varying degrees of matte on your project. Consider how light creates shadows

depending on where it strikes an object and use that as a guide in matting your design.

9. Place your panel in a kiln tray and fire it in the kiln for a second time. The temperature will depend on the type of paint and color you chose to use as a matte.

With these basic steps, you can now create your own stained glass painting. The great thing about this technique is that you can use it on its own to create your panels, or adorn projects you'd assembled with additional designs.

Once you get used to the basic techniques, you can start learning more advanced methods such as silver staining and stamping.

Chapter 4 –Beginner Projects

Stained Glass Box

Materials and Tools:

- Glass – You can choose practically any type of glass you want. However, it is recommended that you select glass that's about 1/8 inch thick. Also, if you will be using different types of glass for each side of the box, remember to choose ones that are of the same thickness.

- Copper foil (7/32" wide. You may also want to use ones that have black backing tso there won't be any copper showing in your project. However, this is not required.)

- Solder (60(tin)/40(lead))
- Copper wire (hinge)
- Flux & brush (or Q-tip)
- Etching paste & squeegee (for frosted effect)
- Contact paper (To use as a stencil for the etching)
- Soldering iron
- Fid or chopstick or roller
- Glass cutter
- Right angle ruler (If you don't have this you can use a regular ruler instead)
- Wire cutters
- Wet sponge
- Exacto knife
- Safety goggles
- Gloves
- Fume extractor
- 1/8" zinc
- Thin chain

What to do:
1. Enlarge the pattern below to the size you want your box to be,

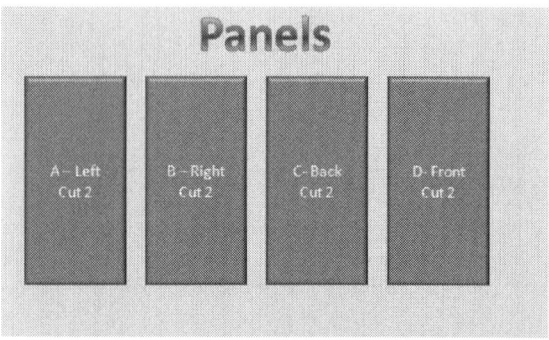

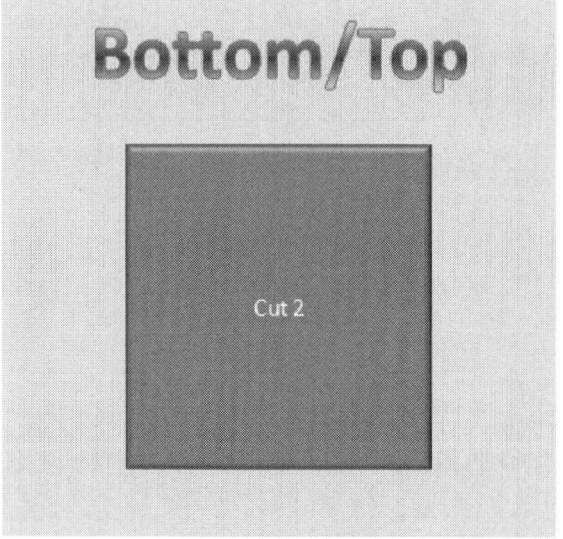

2. Cut out the glass, using the template
3. Take your copper foil and foil all the pieces

4. Take your applicator or Q-tip and apply just enough flux on the foil for soldering

5. Apply a thin solder on the perimeter of the surface of all the pieces

6. Assemble the bottom part of your box by thinly soldering the pieces together. You don't need to add solder, just touch the tip of your iron to the previously thin soldering and press the panels together.

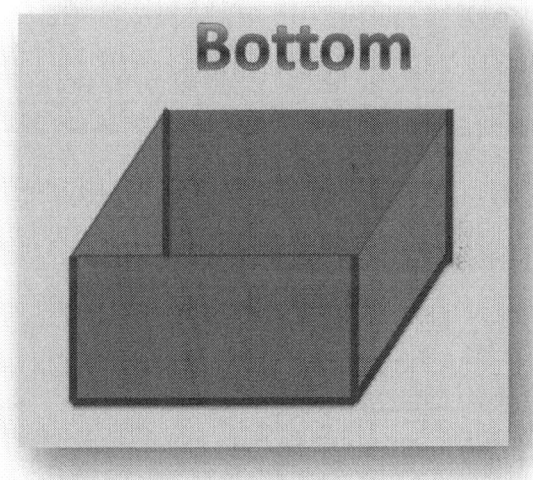

7. Assemble the lid pieces together with a thin solder as well.

8. Handle both parts carefully as the bond is still weak at this point.

9. Check if the bottom and lid parts are of the same size. You can do this by aligning the 2 pieces and see if they fit together. If the panels had been cut and thinly soldered properly there should be no problem. If the pieces do not align, you can go ahead and fix it.

10. Take a piece of 1/8 inch zinc came and slip over the edge of the top and bottom pieces where you will be putting the hinge. Without the zinc, the copper foil may tear away when the hinge is added and used.

11. It is now time to permanently solder the seams of the side panels of the bottom part. For a 3D project, you will need to ensure that you apply solder horizontally. Prop your piece to ensure that the edge you are soldering is facing up.

You can do this by anchoring your piece in a cardboard box filled with crumpled newspaper. This can provide the needed support to keep your working piece in place as you solder.

12. When you're done with the first pass of solder, go back and solder up to the edge.

13. When the side panels have been soldered completely, it's time to reinforce the thin soldering on the bottom panel. Prop the box on a pile of cardboard pieces or a wedge. Make sure that the edge you are

soldering is as flat as possible to prevent the soldering from running out of the hollow.

14. When done. Check all the edges to see if there are any spots or gaps that need to be filled.

15. The final step is to do a beauty pass of solder to ensure that all the seams are uniform and have the bead look.

16. Do the same process for the lid part of the box.

17. With the exterior soldered, use your iron on the inner edges of both the bottom and lid parts. There's no need to add solder. Let the hot iron run along the solder that's already there. When it melts, you can pull on the iron and solder to create the bead look on the inside as well.

18. Inspect both the bottom and lid pieces to check if there are any more sections to be fixed.

19. Take your barrel hinge and resize the tubes to the fit your box.

    a. The barrel hinge has an inner and outer tube. Take these 2 tubes and measure these against your box. Mark where you will be cutting

    b. Cut 2 short pieces off of the outer tube. You should now have three pieces of outer tube, 2 short ones and a long one

    c. Slide the outer tube pieces over the inner tube. Make sure the short pieces are on either side of the long piece.

20. Place the hinge you have just resized on the side that's reinforced by the 1/8" zinc on the bottom part.

21. Apply a little flux on the short outer tubes. Make sure you apply it on the same side. Solder these side outer tubes to the bottom part of the box. Make sure you do not accidentally solder the center tube as well. You can slide a piece of paper under it to serve as a guard.

22. Take the lid part and position the edge with the zinc reinforcement against the hinge and bottom part. Flux the center tube and solder it to the lid. Keep the piece of paper in place so the solder doesn't flow over to the bottom piece.

23. Be careful not to apply too much solder as it might leak into the inner tube and you would have to start all over again.

24. Slide the piece of paper away once you are done soldering and test if the lid opens and

closes. You may need to carefully bend it in place.

25. Take your small link chain and solder the tip to the inside of the front panel of the bottom piece.

26. Open the lid to a little bit over a 90-degree angle. Measure how much chain you will need and cut.

27. Solder the chain to the inside front panel corner of the lid. This will keep your box open when needed without the need to be held.

28. Do a quick test of your box to see if the hinge is working properly and if the lid and bottom are aligned.

29. You can do an etching on the surface of the lid if you wish.

Your basic but beautiful stained glass box is now ready to use or to give as a gift to your loved ones. If this is the first time you work on a 3D stained glass project, don't worry if it tool you a while to complete it. The more you practice and get used to the various techniques the more efficient you will become. You'll certainly be working on more complex projects and patterns soon.

Suncatcher

Materials and Tools:

- Pattern for suncatcher
- Stained glass pieces
- Safety glasses
- Leather or thick rubber gloves
- Glass grinder
- Copper foil
- Lead came

- Glass cutter and oil
- Washable black marker
- Soldering iron
- Flux and applicator or Q-tp
- Lead solder
- Monofilament
- Running pliers
- Copper shears
- Scrap plywood larger than suncatcher pattern
- Hammer and nails
- Steel wool
- Small paintbrushes and rags
- Liquid patina solution
- Copper eye holes

What to Do

1. There are numerous free patterns available online and at your local craft stores. As a beginner, pick ones that have fewer glass pieces as well as basic easy to cut shapes Lay out your pattern on your work surface. Cut the pattern according to the instructions. You'll want to cut each piece on the inside of the lines.

2. Photocopy your pattern so you have one to use as a template and another as a reference when assembling

3. Mark your glass

    a. If you are using transparent glass, place your template underneath your working piece and trace the shapes with a permanent marker.

    b. If you are working with opaque glass, place your paper pattern on top and trace the outline.

    c. Remember to make allowance for the copper foil.

4. Put your safety glasses. Begin scoring and cutting your glass.

5. Break off the pieces you need. Make sure to label these so you know where each one goes. Use your reference pattern as guide.

6. Put your gloves on and grind the edges to remove any rough or jagged corners. Make

sure to keep an eye on your grinder's water reservoir and sponge.

7. Foil the edges of each glass piece.
8. Assemble your glass pieces together on a jig made from came and nails.
9. Take your applicator or Q-tip and apply an even coat of flux on the foil.
10. Solder along the seams on the surface of the suncatcher.
11. Don't forget to do a beauty pass with the solder and iron.
12. Let the solder dry before carefully turning your project.
13. Apply flux on all the seams and solder.
14. Remove the jig you created with the lead came and nails. The suncatcher should now be able to keep its form and shape.
15. Take your copper eyeholes and solder them in place.
16. Once the solder fully cools, clean the glass and solder lines with a brush. Be sure to scrub or brush on the solder to avoid any problems with the patina.
17. Wax your project and buff until there are no more black marks on your cloth or towel. This ensures that there is no oxidation on the solder lines.

18. Apply the patina on your suncatcher with your rag. Keep rubbing until the metal turns dark.
19. The final step is to thread your microfilament (or fishing line) through the copper eye hole and measure the length you need. You are now ready to hang your suncatcher and start enjoying the stunning lighting effect it creates.

Lampshade

Materials and Tools:
- A pattern
- Pencil
- Eraser
- Ruler
- Glass
- Marker
- Vase cap
- Carbon paper

- Light box or a well lit workspace
- Jig materials (nails and wooden batons)
- Glass cutter
- Cutting oil
- Copper foil
- Soldering iron
- Flux and Applicator or Q-tip
- Stretchy Masking Tape (1/2" or ¾")
- Tinned 18 gauge copper wire

What to do:

1. Choose a pattern that you can work with. As a beginner it is best to stay away from designs that have too deep curves and sharp angles. Since you are still getting used to cutting, grinding, foiling and leading, simpler patterns is more advisable.

2. Check the print out of the pattern you will be using. Accuracy is important in making lampshades, so you need to make sure that all the details in the pattern you've chosen are not distorted. The angles need to be symmetrical or else it will be impossible to complete your project.

- Fold your print out in the center and hold it against your lightbox.
- Check if both sides match as they should.
- If they don't fix the angles and areas by erasing and drawing the correct lines and shapes.

3. Once you've chosen and fixed the pattern, Take your print out and copy it onto cardboard with the help of carbon paper. Use a clamp or paper clips to make sure all sheets are steady. Again, it is important to have accurate pattern and templates to be successful in this project.
4. Label the template pieces for easy reference later on. There's no need for you to try to figure it out like a jigsaw puzzle as this will just be downright frustrating.
5. Cut your template. You can use the tips below as guide:

- If you are using pattern shears, these cut a line that's at the same width as the line drawn of a regular ball point pen. So with this tool, you can cut exactly on the marks you'd drawn.
- Regular shears on the other hand may cut at a narrower width. If you

are using a regular pair of scissors, make sure you cut right at the middle of the lines you'd marked. If you cut on the inside of the line, your glass pieces may be smaller than the needed size. If you cut on the outside of the line, the pieces may be too big.

6. When you have cut all the template pieces, lay this on your paper printout. The outlines should be visible around each of your template cut-outs.
7. Take a board or tile that's about 2-3 inches larger that the pattern you have chosen. Tape the printed out pattern on the board with strips of masking tape. This will serve as your guide when assembling each panel.

8. Create a jig by nailing down a wooden baton or strip of wood on each side of the pattern. Make sure that you align these properly with the bordering lines of the pattern. If the jig isn't accurate then your panel will not be accurate as well.

9. Score and cut the glass you will need for one panel using the cardboard templates you'd prepared

10. Foil the glass pieces

11. With your applicator or Q-tip apply flux on the foil to prepare it for soldering.

12. Tack solder (applying a thin coat of solder) the seams and set aside.

13. Assemble the remaining panels.

14. When all of the panels have been built, it's time to do a permanent solder on the seams. Start with the front and carefully go over all the seams. Make sure you even out the sections where you did a tack solder earlier to get that even beaded look for the entire seam.

15. Once the front is done, turn the panel over so you can work on the back side. Solder the seams. Again, make sure that you even out where you did tack solders earlier.

16. Do not apply any solder on the glass edges. You will work on them later on.

17. With a brush and sudsy cleaner, wash your soldered panels. Wipe with a dry paper towel. Keep rubbing with the towel until no more black rubs off.

18. Once the panels are completely dry, it's time to assemble your lampshade. This will basically be like completing a jigsaw puzzle. Don't worry about having to arrange it in an upright position. Just lay the panels flat on your worktable. Also,

the panels don't need to be completely flat against each other. There may be some slight gaps in the middle. You can fix those later with solder.

19. Take your masking tape and attach the panels to each other. Tape the panels together with the stretchy masking tape. Make sure that the tape goes all the way around the panels. This will make putting it into shape a lot easier later on.

Apply the tape in three different sections,

- At the top of the panels just a little bit below the top edge copper foiling.
- At the middle of the panels.
- At the bottom of the panels just above the copper foiling.

When your tape has gone around to the starting point, make sure to overlap and leave about a 2-3 inch extra. Think of it as the end of a shoelace that you will be using later on to keep the lampshade in shape.

20. Lift the taped project by sliding your hand middle fingers on the hole that's now at the top. (hole created by the panels being put side by side.)

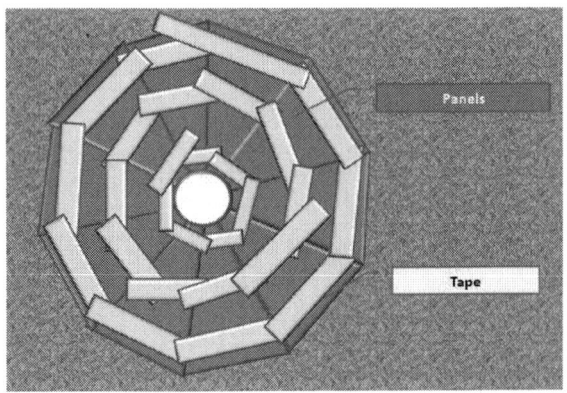

21. Press down on the tape tail to keep the lampshade in shape.
22. Your shade should now look like a half open umbrella (or a fully opened one depending on the pattern you are using). Turn the lampshade upside down. Since the tape is only on the top, expect your project to slightly change shape as gravity takes over. Don't worry if it opens up a little bit more, this is the shape you want it to have.
23. Tack solder the inside seams. This will keep it in shape when you take off the masking tape.
24. Once the solder cools, you can flip it right side back up. Apply some solder on the top just above the masking tape. Be careful not to get solder on the tape.
25. It is now time to make sure that you're lampshade is level, meaning the bottom

will lay flat on the surface. If it doesn't, it will certainly look wonky when you place it on the lamp.

26. After all the seams are tack soldered, it is time to carefully remove the masking tape. The lampshade is still fragile at this point so keep it sitting upright and avoid applying too much pressure on it.

27. Take the tinned wire and solder it on the top edges. You can try to bend the wire with your hands but using a pair of nose pliers will make it a lot easier. You can measure how much wire you need prior to soldering. Clothes pins (the spring type) are going to be handy at this point. You can use it to anchor the wire so it doesn't go all over the place while you're soldering.

28. Take the vase cap and tin it.

29. Lay the lamp vase cap on top of the lampshade. Make sure that it is level and then tack solder it in different spots

30. Carefully place the lampshade on its side and solder the inside seams. Make sure that the seam you are soldering is as horizontal as possible to avoid the solder from running. Don't forget to seam around the edges of the vase cap as well.

31. Tin the inside of the bottom edges.

32. Prop up your project. You can purchase a lamp wedgie that will make this a lot easier. However, you can use other things around the home for this. You can fill a shallow cardboard box with crumpled newspapers or prop the lampshade on bottles or books

33. Take your soldering iron and solder the outer seams. Make sure that the seam you are working on is as flat or as horizontal as possible. You don't want to be chasing after rolling solder. Be careful when you're turning the lampshade to get to another seam as you might touch hot solder. This can be extremely painful.

34. When you finish with the seams outside, leave it to dry for a few minutes.

35. Check all the solder lines on both the interior and exterior surfaces. Do a touch up on any parts that may need filling in.

36. Turn your lampshade upside down.

37. Take your tinned wire and solder it onto the bottom edge. Make sure you have a pair of nose pliers so you can shape the wire properly. Anchor the wire to the lampshade with spring clothespins.

38. When you have attached the wire to the bottom edge, solder over it to give it a clean beaded look.

Working on this project may take a while. However, once you master the techniques needed, your future projects won't be quite as difficult to complete.

Conclusion

Thank you again for purchasing this book, I hope you found it enjoyable to read while you gained both knowledge and inspiration!

The next step is to start practicing the different techniques and methods described in this book. Remember, stained glass crafting isn't easy but once you begin to master it, it will certainly be worth your while.

Despite the numerous tools and materials mentioned within the book, don't get overwhelmed with the amount of shopping (and the costs) you will have to do. Start off with the basic and necessary materials before investing in the more expensive (and sometimes optional) stuff.

Good Luck on your journey to creating stunning works stained glass pieces!

Manufactured by Amazon.ca
Bolton, ON